100 YEARS OF CHANGE:

The "hub" of the Danish community, the DBS Hall (Danish Brotherhood Society) was not only used for meetings, it was the center of social activities in the community. Dances, birthday parties, anniversary celebrations, showers, school functions and receptions were held here, and attended by my grandparents, parents, and siblings. My children had wedding receptions and many celebrations at the hall, and their families still gather here for Krebs Christmas. It seemed fitting for the cover of my book. (There is more on this in chapter 7)

100 YEARS OF CHANGE:

The Life of Margaret Mary (Nielsen) Krebs

Growing Up in Trufant and Howard City, MI

Margaret Krebs

ISBN: 978-1-7362303-8-1
Book design by Jessica Angerstein (jessica@dezinermama.com)
Published and printed in the United States

To My Dear Children –

Love you all
so very much,
Mother

TABLE OF

Contents

Prologue...i

Chapter 1: Grandpa and Grandma Nielsen.. 1

Chapter 2: Grandpa and Grandma White.. 7

Chapter 3: Mother and Dad 11

Chapter 4: Life and Home was Hard Work... 23

Chapter 5: Grandpa White Enriched our Lives..................................... 33

Chapter 6: It Wasn't All Work; We Did Have Some Fun! 37

Chapter 7: The Trufant Community 43

Chapter 8: My Education and Career... 57

Chapter 9: LeMoyne 69

Chapter 10: Lots of Real Estate 79

Chapter 11: Founding Christ the King & St. Francis de Sales Church 83

Chapter 12: Fond Memories... 87

Chapter 13: My Siblings 103

Chapter 14: My Children 121

Acknowledgements... 131

About the Author 133

Margaret Mary (Nielsen) Krebs

PROLOGUE

I am writing this book to describe what my life was like growing up in Trufant and Howard City, and the tremendous changes that have taken place over the past 100 years. I am 98 at this time, and my granddaughter offered to help me write my story (Karen Cornell, wife of my self-proclaimed "favorite" grandson, Rob). After being hospitalized in 2021, this book was a wonderful distraction to help me get through that challenging time. We have had a great time capturing these stories.

I hope that as you read this, you will try to picture day to day life the way it was in the early 1900's. It was a hard life, but we were happy and enjoyed the simple pleasures, particularly time with family. We survived disease, war, and the Great Depression. If there is one thing that I would love to see you take away from this book, it would be that life is full of ups and downs, and you can overcome life's many challenges. For me it was family, dear friends, and my faith that got me through the hard times. I'm grateful for all the wonderful times we have had together over the years. I have had an amazing life full of so many blessings.

Margaret Krebs

Karen Sophia and Jens Christian Nielsen

CHAPTER 1

Grandpa and Grandma
Nielsen

My grandparents on my father's side, Jens Christian Nielsen (born June 12, 1860) and Karen Sophia (born July 19, 1856) came over to the United States on the SS Geiser when they were 23 and 27 years old.

SS Geiser

Through her research into our family history, Alger's wife, Nancy Nielsen, shared information on the SS Geiser that highlights just how hard and dangerous it was to make the voyage:

"*The SS Geiser was an iron ship built in 1881. It cost approximately $300,000 to build, and her net register was 1000 tons. She was 313 feet long and traveled at a speed of 12 knots per hour. Accommodations were provided for fifty first-class passengers, fifty second-class passengers, and 900 third-class passengers. There were three hospitals aboard with bunks for forty patients. Documents indicate that Jens and Karen departed Copenhagen on the SS Geiser on May 11, 1883, and arrived in New York City on June 2, 1883 (it was only the second voyage taken). They were "steerage class", which means they worked to pay their way. In its fifth year of operation, the SS Geiser was in collision with the SS Thingvalla on a foggy day, August 14, 1888, about five miles off Sable Island, Newfound Land. The SS Geiser sank within five minutes of the accident, where 79 passengers and 26 members of the crew lost their lives.*"

Upon arriving in New York City, they travelled by train to Michigan, carrying their belongings in a wooden box. They made the remainder of their trip via horse and buggy. There are no pictures of Jens and Karen at this time, and no one knows whether they fell in love in Denmark, or on the ship coming to the US. We do know they were married on September 15, 1883, in Gowen, MI where they settled and built a home. They had eight children: Walter (died soon after birth), Lars Walter, Methora, Lind, Carl (my father, born August 31, 1890), Hans, Agnes (died at age two), and Levi.

I have few memories of Grandma and Grandpa Nielsen, as I was five years old when grandpa died (January 19, 1928) and six when grandma died (May 30, 1929). I do remember that they always brought candy corn and pink peppermints when they came to our home. They came to help cut seed potatoes when it was planting time. They were hard-working and supportive, always willing to help when needed.

They were hard-working and supportive, always willing to help when needed.

Grandpa and Grandma Nielson in front of their home:
presumably Lars, Methora, Lind and Carl

I remember once when I was at their home in Trufant, I got spanked by my mom for pulling the chains on the grandfather clock. I was not supposed to touch it.

Grandpa died at 68 years of age and grandma at 73. Both are buried in Little Denmark Cemetery in Gowen, MI.

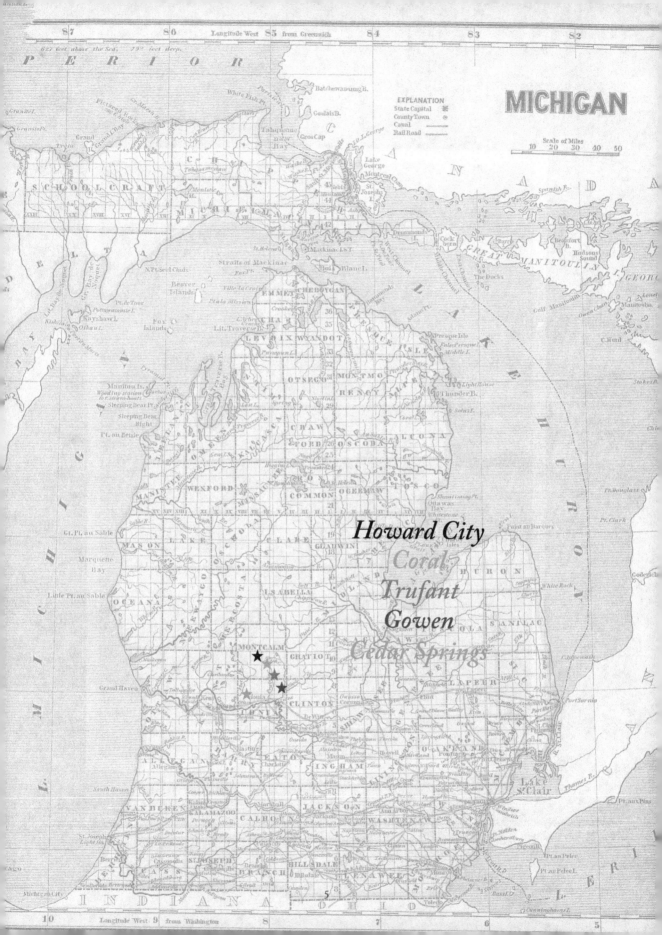

MICHIGAN

EXPLANATION
State Capital
County Town
Canal
Rail Road

Scale of Miles
10   20   30   40   50

627 feet above the Sea,   792 feet deep.

Howard City

Coral

Trufant

Gowen

Cedar Springs

Grandpa White and his daughters, Etta and Belva (mother)

Grandpa and Grandma White

My grandparents on my mother's side were Benson White (born 1862) and Calla Lily Robinson (born 1873). Her great great-grandparents were Rix Robinson (acknowledged as being the first white American of Kent County) and Sippy Quay. Rix Robinson was widely recognized for his role in the settlement of Michigan; at one point, according to historical records, he owned over 65% of Michigan. There is a stone monument in downtown Ada in his honor.

I am not sure when they were married, but Benson and Calla had two daughters, Belva and Marietta (whom we always called Etta). In his younger years, Grandpa White lived in Ada, and he took people and their goods by raft from smaller rivers to the Grand River. This was an important way for people to transport their goods. Presumably that is where he met Calla Lily.

My mother, Belva, was born on July 25, 1891, and Etta was born in 1893. Calla Lily left Grandpa for another man when the girls were about thirteen and eleven years old. We never heard another word about her. Grandpa was a carpenter and needed to work. During that time, men would not be left to raise young children on their own. The girls were sent to St. John's orphanage in Grand Rapids, where they were cared for by nuns. Mother learned many skills and this is where she developed her strong Catholic faith. She was a life-long, devout Catholic. She would grow up to be an excellent cook, seamstress, housekeeper and teacher.

Calla Lily

Sadly, Etta died of typhoid fever when she was fourteen while staying at the convent. She is buried in Old Maple Valley Cemetery with Calla (Calla was buried next to Etta later in life, and we found their graves when we were much older).

Grandpa White worked as a carpenter with his brother George, whom he lived with in Trufant after he separated from Calla. They lived in the home across from the doctor's office. They built many homes and barns together. They were both known for their expert craftsmanship.

Grandpa was a great part of my life. He was always there with a smile and a helping hand. I don't remember him ever having a bad thing to say about anyone.

Sometime later when George passed away, Grandpa White moved in with Belva (my mother) on the farm, so he didn't have to live alone. He always lived with us from the time I can remember. He never spoke of his wife. He was a quiet, gentle man and was always there to care for us.

First Communion of Etta and Belva

Belva and Carl, my mother and father, on their wedding day

CHAPTER THREE

Mother and Dad

Mother graduated from Trufant high school (it went through grade 10) and then went one year at County Normal. This allowed her to earn her teaching certificate. She taught at the Settlement School near Gowen for a year, and then at Burley School, three miles north of Howard City where the flea markets are held. Mother used to take the train from Gowen to Howard City (Burley School), stay there during the week, and return on weekends. That's where she met Dad. He also graduated from high school, and they married in 1914, raising a family of nine children: Lloyd, Ken, Frieda, Agnes, Carl (Boots), Belva, Margaret, Alger, and Rit. Sadly, their tenth child, Patricia, was stillborn.

Carl, Belva and 9 children – 50th Wedding Anniversary

Family picture, 50th wedding anniversary

No. 5478   # Marriage License.   191_4_

_____Montcalm_____ **County, Michigan.**

To any Person legally authorized to solemnize marriage.

Greeting:

Marriage May be Solemnized Between

Mr.___Carl Ferdnand Nielsen___ and M_iss Belva White_____,

affidavit having been filed in this office, as provided by Public Act No. 128, Laws of 1887,
as amended, by which it appears that said

_____Carl Ferdnand Nielsen_____ is____24_____years of age,

color is__White____, residence is_____Trufant_____, and birthplace was

_____Gowen_____, occupation is_____Carpenter_____, father's name

_Christian Nielsen___, and mother's maiden name was___Sophia Nielsen_____,

has been previously married__non time___; and that said__Belva White_____

is_23_ years of age, color is_White___, residence is___Trufant_____and

birthplace was___Trufant_____, occupation is____School Teacher, father's

name____Benson White_____, and mother's maiden name was___Kettie_____

___Robenson_____, and who has been previously married__non time___, and whose

maiden name was_____-_____-____, and whose_____PARENT'S OR GUARDIAN'S____consent,

in case she has not attained the age of eighteen years, has been filed in my office.

In Witness Whereof, I have hereunto attached my
hand and the seal of Montcalm_____County,
Michigan, this_23_ day of_October_____,
A. D. 191_4_

L. S.

Ho W Taylor
COUNTY CLERK.

Certificate of Marriage.

Between Mr._Carl Nielsen_____ and Miss _Belva White_

I Hereby Certify that, in accordance with the above license, the persons herein mentioned
were joined in marriage by me, at _Maple Valley_County of _Montcalm_,
Michigan, on the _28_ day of _October_, A. D. 191_4_, in the
presence of _Hans Paul Poulsen_, of _Trufant_,
and _Catherine Coady_, of _Coral_,
as witnesses.

D J Wynne
NAME OF MAGISTRATE OR CLERGYMAN.
Priest
OFFICIAL TITLE.

☛ THIS DUPLICATE must be delivered by the person solemnizing
marriage to one of the parties joined in marriage.

Dad bought a dairy farm, but his business was mostly buying and distributing potatoes. He had a potato cellar in Trufant next to the elevator across from the hardware store. He stored the potatoes until it was time to bag and distribute them. Sometimes the boys would grab a few friends and help Dad sort and bag the potatoes, loading 100 lb. bags. This was hard work. Potato cellars were covered in dirt to keep them insulated. In the winter, fires were lit to keep the cellars warm, just around 40, so the potatoes would not freeze. Men would stay up all night tending to the potato cellars, often drinking and playing cards.

The potato truck was also our mode of transportation to church, as it could carry all of us!

Dad had a potato truck which he used to get potatoes to the flea markets in Grand Rapids and Muskegon. I have many memories of the poor road conditions during my childhood. I remember calling in the horses to help pull people out when they got stuck. I also remember there was a big hill in Rockford that was impassable at times depending on the weather. Dad couldn't always get his truck up that hill when it was full of potatoes, especially if it had been raining. There was also a rubber shortage, so tires were hard to come by; everyone had to patch them, which made travel very slow. He also shipped potatoes by train to Detroit and Chicago. The potato truck was also our mode of transportation to church, as it could carry all of us!

Grandpa White with workers in front of Nielsen potato truck

Potato cellar by railroad track

Dad bought a small parcel of land on the northeast side of Trufant Lake. It was land locked, so he had to build a road to access it. He built two log houses and another home that he sold. That road is called Nielsen Drive today. Mom thought it was a gravel pit!

Later, Dad bought the Maple Valley Tavern from John Quigg. There was a bar on one side and a restaurant on the other side. Mother was the cook, and I helped in the summer when I was home. One time Dad asked me to go help serve beer, but just sixteen at the time, I told him I didn't know anything about beer and asked for another job. I was not going to be a bartender! The next summer when I came home, I got to be the boss for two weeks. Dad also had two poker rooms.

Alger, Edson, Kenneth, Benson, Belva, Carl, Rit, Ruby

The Old Farm

Larger Farmhouse

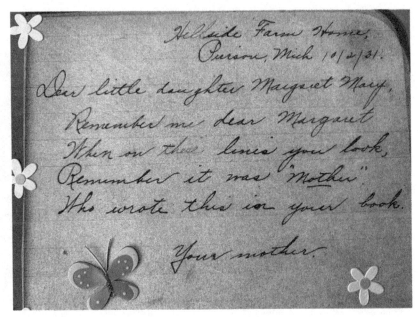

Note from mother in autograph book

Dad was very interested in politics and was a passionate democrat. He made us listen to the news, so we knew what was going on in the world. Cribbage was another of Dad's passions—we all grew up knowing how to play because Dad always wanted to have someone to play with. Rit swears he could play at five years old. We were very close with Dad's family. We had lots of visits with uncles, aunts, and cousins. There were picnics at Long Lake, and many Nielsen Reunions.

Cribbage was another of Dad's passions—we all grew up knowing how to play because Dad always wanted to have someone to play with.

Belva (mother) with her students

Belva (mother) posing with teacher friends after playing basketball

Trufant
Public Schools
1913-1914

Faculty

GEO. E. BERSETTE, Principal
ETHEL C. CRAME, Grammar
WILLIAM SIMMONS, Intermediate
BELVA WHITE, Primary

Board of Education

JOHN REYNOLDS, President
CARL CHRISTENSEN, Secretary
CARL F. HANSEN, Treasurer
CHRIS H. LARSEN, Trustee
PETER JENSEN, Trustee

Frieda, Agnes, Carl (Boots),
Margaret, Lloyd (in wagon),
Ken (behind Lloyd) and
Belva - 1925

Frieda, Ken, Agnes (baby buggy) and Lloyd

Later in her life my mother was having trouble with her legs because of "bad veins" and went to have surgery. Dr. Bunce said it was one of the bloodiest surgeries he had ever seen. A nurse came over and wanted Mom to get out of bed, but she had a lot of gas, was very weak and didn't want to get up. She had a blood clot from her surgery which caused a heart attack and she passed away the following day. It was such a shock. Everyone had been home to see her. I was teaching at the Lutheran church and Boots came to get me. He said I needed to go and visit Mom but didn't tell me she died until we got home. She was 63. Dad had a stroke at 66, but really died of a broken heart. Frieda was taking care of him, and they expected him to recover. He was mad at Dr. Bunce and never got over mother dying. Through all their ups and downs, Mom and Dad had a close relationship and a good life together.

Mom and Dad had a close relationship and a good life together.

Freida, Lloyd, Boots, Agnes and Ken with Grandpa White and their dog, Sport

CHAPTER FOUR

Life at Home was Hard Work

Growing up on a farm was a hard and busy life. Mother and Dad built the first house, where Lloyd, Ken, Frieda, Agnes, and Boots were born. In later years, Frieda and her husband, Clair, lived in that house when they got married.

The larger farmhouse where I grew up was built by Grandpa White and his brother, George, on the same piece of property. It was a very nice house with four bedrooms. Belva, myself, Alger, and Rit were all born here. There was still no electricity in rural areas when I grew up, so we did not have electricity on the farm and used kerosene lamps and one gasoline lantern for light. Chimneys had to be washed often as the kerosene blackened the lamp shades. We had a two-hole outhouse and used Sears & Roebucks catalogs for toilet paper.

We had an icebox to keep things cold in the summer. In the winter, the men would go to the lake and cut ice. They used saws and ice tongs and would carry the bricks home via horse and wagon to the cement building where the ice blocks were stored; they were wrapped in sawdust to keep them from melting. Everyone purchased the ice blocks in the summer, and they would last about a week in our ice box at home.

Ice removal on Muskalonge (Trufant) Lake to be stored until needed in the summer

CUTTING ICE ON MUSKALONGE (TRUFANT) LAKE IN THE 1930's.
PICTURE OF THE ACTUAL CUTTING, SENDING BLOCKS OF ICE UP A RAMP TO THE WAITING
WAGONS, THE ICE WAS THEN HAULED TO THE 'ICE HOUSE', (THE CEMENT BLOCK BUILDING
BEHIND THE PHARMACY), UNLOADED, PACKED IN SAW DUST OR STRAW UNTIL SUMMER TIME.
THEN PEOPLE WOULD PURCHASE THE ICE FOR THEIR 'ICE BOXES'.
THIS WAS BEFORE ELECTRICITY AND REFRIGERATION.

The four of us girls had to sleep in one bedroom, and the mattress was a tick filled with straw. When we threshed the wheat, the straw was used to fill the tick. It started out very high but it soon packed down to form our mattress. Three boys slept in one room: Ken, Lloyd and Boots. When Rit was young, he used to sleep with the girls and we were always talking. He would say he had a headache because he wanted us to be quiet and go to sleep. As he got older, Rit usually slept with Grandpa. He liked that because that bedroom was next to the kitchen stove and it was warm. He didn't like sleeping with the boys because their room was cold! They would heat stones and put them by their feet. Alger had to sleep in the dining room on a day bed. It was a colder room but he always said he had plenty of quilts and blankets to keep him warm; Mom made two quilts each year to help in that regard.

In the younger years, Frieda and I were always together, and Agnes and Belva were very close. As we got older Agnes and Frieda wanted to sleep together so they could talk about teenage girl things and share secrets! Mom said I had to sleep with Belva and I cried and cried! Mom told me she would make me a new nightgown to help console me. I was always afraid of the dark and sometimes the girls would blow out the light and shut the door to scare me and hear me cry. To this day I don't like the bedroom door completely closed.

Mother baked many loaves of bread every day, and canned fruits and vegetables all summer for winter use. We had a huge garden and our own strawberry and raspberry patches. We had cows, pigs, chickens, and two horses: Pete and Jim. We also had an Arabian horse to ride named Daisy. She was very flighty and would try to bite us when putting the bit in her mouth. You had to keep the reins tight while riding her or she'd reach around and bite your leg! She was really fast when she headed for home, where she knew she would get some oats.

We had cows, pigs, chickens, and
two horses: Pete and Jim.

We had a windmill that piped water into the house. Then it flowed out to the barn, so we could get water to all the animals. It was all gravity except where it came from the pump. Sometimes the wind didn't blow enough and we would take the gasoline engine from the washer to the pump to get water going. Grandpa White helped with all of these things.

1950 Potato pickers: Pat, Alice, Nan and Jimmy

We all helped with the chores on the farm. Mom made lists of jobs for us and changed them each week, although we could swap if our siblings agreed. We washed up in the sink first. Then the girls swept the floors, pumped the water, helped with the washing (getting water in the tubs), and hung up clothes on the line. We also helped with cooking and the dishes. The boys did farm chores: they milked the cows, put milk in cans so the milk truck could take the cans to the creamery, and fed the animals (about eight cows, two horses, chickens, and two pigs). They had to chop wood for the stoves. They also had to clean the buckets each day that we used to go to the bathroom at night (yuck!). There was not much downtime living on a farm.

We all helped with the chores on the farm.

Ken and Dad would get up early to take potatoes to the market in Muskegon, so he would take an afternoon nap. One time, Rit slammed the screen door and was spanked for waking up Dad.

Dad was a strict disciplinarian but had to be with such a large family to raise. Mom always had a kind word for everyone.

Mother was an excellent cook and seamstress; she made all our clothes. When we got flour, it came in sacks that had different designs, and everyone used them to make dresses and clothes. The first time she used a zipper, she made Lloyd a zip-up jacket when he was going to college. Mom had to cook for 12 people, and as soon as we could stand on the stool we had to help with dishes. She was very kind and always had time to go out and help someone else. People called on her because she was helpful, very intelligent, and good at everything she did. She made six or seven loaves of bread every day. We didn't have choices for breakfast; you had to have oatmeal or cream of wheat. Occasionally we had pancakes and bacon (from our pigs), and sometimes we had potatoes, bacon, and eggs. We didn't have much money, but we had a lot of food.

As soon as we could stand on the stool we had to help with dishes.

We also separated the milk and sold cream, and churned our own butter. We gave the skim milk to the pigs, and I could never stand drinking skim milk because it reminded me of the curdled milk that was in the pig trough. One time I got spanked because I didn't put the churn lid on tight and when I turned it, I spilled all the cream. We had a cream separator in the basement of our house, and we sold the cream, butter, eggs, and milk at Hans Rasmussen's store, trading them for sugar, beans, rice, and flour. We loved going there on Saturday nights, and sometimes got a five-cent ice cream. That was such a treat.

Threshing days were long and busy. That was when we got our oats and wheat processed. We'd cook up lots of food to feed the neighbors who came over to help. In those times, everyone helped each other. They would always show up to help right around lunchtime because everyone wanted a taste of Mom's cooking.

In those times, everyone helped each other.

I hated haying season because we'd have to be up in the hay loft and mow away the hay (Hot! Hot! Hot!). We brought the hay via horse to the barn. A pully system pulled the hay up, dumping it into the loft. We were always making contraptions to get things done. Later we liked to jump in the hay.

Hauling Hay

People often joke about the adage, "When I was young, I walked two miles each way to get to school," but we truly did! Blake school was two miles from our house, and it was particularly hard in the winter because we didn't have many warm clothes. Everyone (including neighbors) walked to school together.

Belva remembers our poor decision to take a short cut through a farmer's field. Not only did the farmer chase us off the property, but so did his bull.

Everyone (including neighbors) walked to school together.

When mother had her last baby, only Belva and I were home, approximately ten and eleven at the time. Dad had taken Frieda and Agnes to a dance at Pine Lake. Mother told Belva and I to go get the oil cloth from the kitchen table and put it under her on the bed, get a sheet, and fetch as many newspapers as we could find. Then she told us to call Dr. Bunce. Belva had to go get the neighbor, Elvie Larsen, to help. There was no way to contact Dad, but when he came home, he put us right to bed. After the baby was stillborn, mother said, "God is telling me nine children is enough." Frieda dressed the baby and put her in a shoebox. The boys and grandpa made a small wooden casket for her; Dr. Bunce told Mom and Dad to bury her in the orchard.

Grandpa White

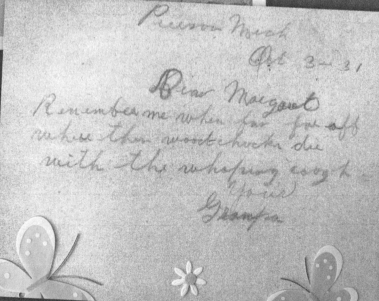

Note from Grandpa White, 1931

CHAPTER FIVE

Grandpa White Enriched Our Lives

Grandpa White helped Mom with the odd jobs around the farm, while Dad was working on the potato business. It was very helpful to have another man around. Grandpa was loved by everyone and was a huge influence on us all. I never remember him being angry or raising his voice.

Grandpa was loved by everyone and was a huge influence on us all.

Grandpa was our babysitter when my parents went dancing or fishing. He kept the gasoline engine running on the washing machine. He kept the smokehouse going and helped butcher the animals. He cured the hams and sausages. Since we didn't have refrigeration, smoking the meat was very important. He built tables, chairs, and porch swings. He made our family table, which was very long so that it sat all twelve of us. We had six chairs and several benches, and an oil cloth on that table which made it easy to clean. We didn't buy toys, but grandpa made us stilts, wagons, sleds, and any wooden toys we wanted. He could repair just about anything.

> ## *We didn't buy toys, but grandpa made us stilts, wagons, sleds, and any wooden toys we wanted.*

Sometimes Grandpa drank in the basement when Mom and Dad were gone. Alger remembered hearing the tinkling sound of glass and finding grandpa counting his empty beer bottles. Upon being caught in this condition, he said, "I think I had too much! I'm a stinker!" Grandpa made his own beer, and Alger had his first beer with Grandpa when he was eight or nine, after cutting hay. Grandpa was not a big drinker and I never remember seeing him drink too much.

We lost our farm during the Great Depression when I was sixteen years old. It was sold by auction, and we moved back to Grandpa White's house in Trufant (Dad bought it from him). That was the first time we had electricity and indoor plumbing. I am proud to say that around this time, Grandpa wanted to become a Catholic, and I was his "Godparent" when he was baptized at home. That is such a special memory.

Grandpa White and his daughter, Belva

Nielson Wins Berlin Race

Dick Nielson, 25-year-old Trufant farmer, Saturday night won the feature, 25-lap stock car race before 3,600 persons at Berlin raceway.

Nielson fought off Ed Vander Laan and Bob Knight, veteran Grand Rapids drivers, who finished second and third, respectively.

Wild Bill Wiltse set a new track record when he negotiated a lap in :13.8 seconds during time trials, more than a second faster than the old record held by Knight.

In the 10-lap speed sprints winners were VanderLaan, Art Eyers, Sam Ash, and Bud Meyering, all of Grand Rapids.

Bill Rider of Grand Rapids won the fast-car dash and Tommy Lane of Muskegon the Australian pursuit race. Ayers and Elmer Lovett of Grand Rapids each won 15-lap semi-final races.

WINS FIRST OF THE YEAR-Dick Nielsen, Trufant, holds checkered flag emblematic of victory in season's opening feature race at Berlin raceway Saturday night. Nielson won the 25-lap feature before 3,600 fans.

CHAPTER SIX

It Wasn't All Work;
We Did Have Some Fun!

We enjoyed walking across the fields to swim in Picnic Lake. Mom and Dad loved to fish there. We would go with an older sibling or with our whole family. Our swimming lesson was to get shoved off the dock and have to swim. Boots "taught" me to swim! Dad built a small changing room. Mom wouldn't let us go if it was too hot, so sometimes we put cool water on the thermometer. When our friends Bruce Hansen and Kendall Chapell came over to go swimming, Belva and I would often stay home so we could ride their bikes. We never did have bikes of our own.

> ## Our swimming lesson was to get shoved off the dock and have to swim.

When I was very young, I liked to light matches. We had a gas stove to use instead of the big range. I'd climb up and get the matches and light some papers.

Agnes caught me one time when I had a little fire right next to my dress. She teased me for many years about saving me and my fascination with fire.

Growing up, we all sat around the radio and listened to Gabriel Heatter's news program, and "Lum and Abner," a comedy program. Everyone had to sit still and listen. Dad always called Frieda's sons, Jerry Feutz "Lum" and Norman Feutz "Abner". That name stuck for Norman his whole life. We all loved listening to Lum and Abner and laughing together. Mom and Dad liked listening to the news and wanted us to know what was going on in the world.

We all loved listening to Lum and Abner and laughing together.

Christmas holidays and birthdays were always fun but gifts were simple. I remember getting a Celluloid doll, and Belva getting a diary. We usually got socks, underwear, or things we needed.

On Tuesday nights we had free movie shows outside in the summer. This was a big deal! We also saw five cent shows in Coral in a field. You got candy bars, three for ten cents. Depression years were hard. There were 25 cent shows in Greenville. People rode together and chipped in for gas. As we got older, that was where we met boys and would sit with them. We always had lots of kids around to play games such as "Kick the Can", "Spin the Bottle," baseball, or football.

Many people still had horses and buggies when I was young. In the winter we used the horse and sleigh and kept warm with blankets. I was about six years old when we got a car. Grandpa White had a Model T Ford pick-up truck, and we all wanted to ride in it. I remember one time we wanted to ride into town with Grandpa but he told us we couldn't go with him. Alger and I grabbed on the back of the truck and hung on as far as we could before we let go and skinned up our knees. He never knew or we would have been in so much trouble! It was a long walk home.

The playground at school had a giant classic merry-go-round where you grabbed the handles and ran around in circles before jumping on. We loved playing on it and found a way to hop on often.

Nielsen family wins "Largest Family" at Coral 4-H Days. Nine in a row:
Lloyd, Ken, Frieda, Agnes, Carl (Boots), Belva, Margaret, Alger, and mother holding Rit

We used to play a lot of softball in the yard and ride the horses for fun. We made our own wooden bats, and I remember Alger making his own glove from a piece of leather. The boys used boxing gloves to box in the barn. Although we were not allowed, we liked to walk across the beam in the barn. It was fun but a bit dangerous as one time I fell and received a concussion. Another time, Rit was trying to get a cat off the beam and fell and was knocked out. He started throwing up, but never told anyone so mom and dad thought he had the flu. He knew he would get in trouble for being on the beam.

> *We made our own wooden bats, and I remember Alger making his own glove from a piece of leather.*

Baseball was a big sport during this time. Rit pitched in high school and struck out 17 in one game. He and Alger played ball for the Trufant Independents. Rit pitched and Alger was catcher. Dad managed the team, and they traveled around to other cities to play. When the game was in Trufant, we always had a big crowd. Opposing teams loved coming to Trufant because we took up a collection and the winning team got 50% and the losing team got 40% (the remainder went to the ballpark). Everyone came out to watch the games as there were some very gifted players that were so fun to watch. Rit even took a job at the Tool and Die Company so he could play on their baseball team. Tommy Conners was a great local pitcher.

Alger played basketball all four years in high school. In ninth grade, Dad would say he could go through other guys' legs because he was little and fast.

Reunion at Lincoln Lake, 1943
Top: Connie Richardson. Albert Nielsen, Norman Feutz, Alice Feutz, Nancy Nielsen, Deanna Richardson,
Patty Nielsen, Jerry Feutz. Front row: Jim Feutz, Gary Richardson, Barbara Ludtke, Judy Feutz, Mary Nielsen.
Very front, crying is John Stout

St. Clara's Catholic Church, attended during childhood

Emory Trufant

The Trufant Community

Early settlers came to the Trufant area in the mid 1850's and cleared land for farming. The first tract of land that would become Trufant, in Maple Valley township, Michigan, was granted by the United States government to Emory Trufant in 1854. This land was recorded along the southwest side of Trufant Lake. He built a sawmill in 1871, and soon after a steam sawmill that would allegedly be the first in this country. Shingle mills and planning mills were operating in the area employing eighty men.

Farming was very important to many of the Danish settlers. Early settlers removed the pine trees to sell the lumber and plant crops. The pine trees in the Trufant area were massive, leaving behind huge stumps that were initially removed by hand, and later by machine. Settlers cultivated the land and planted their crops, using the stumps with a prickly root system as fences to enclose their property and keep the animals from wandering off. Trufant was known for this practice and was later named the "Stump Fence Capital of the US", even the world! You can still see stumps around the perimeter of yards today.

Stump fencing roadside

Stump fence excavator

The Railroad

As the stump fences popped up around Trufant, so did many other businesses. The railroad was built through Trufant and quickly became an important connection to transport potatoes, dry goods, lumber, and various other materials to larger cities. Railroad tracks were laid in the late 1800's and began running in the early 1900's. The Pere Marquette Railroad Company, which operated a greater mileage in Montcalm County than any other system, operated a line from Ionia to Howard City, where it connected with The Grand Rapids & Indiana Railroad through Greenville, Gowen, Trufant, and Coral. Through various lines, people and products could travel to Detroit, Grand Rapids, and even to Chicago. Throughout our childhood, we all loved watching the trains going in and out of town to see what they were carrying.

High bridge of the railroad tracks, a popular place to watch the trains

The DBS Hall

The DBS Hall was the social hub of Trufant when I grew up. It was built by the Danish Brotherhood Society, which was formed in communities where significant numbers of Danes had settled. The DBS provided a forum for nurturing Danish culture and language as well as provided financial assistance to members in case of death or illness. Inside the hall, there was a room upstairs where meetings were held. Only lodge members could go into that room, which made all of us kids very curious about it! The men spoke Dane there for many years to keep their language. They discussed issues and everyone helped each other. Mother joined the "Rebecca's Lodge," which was a similar organization for Danish women in a building downtown.

We always had dances at the DBS Hall, typically once a week on a Friday or Saturday night. Mother and Dad loved to dance, as did all of us kids. When we were very young, we played or slept in a room while the adults danced. There was square dancing, waltzing, and Danish dancing. Dancing was a big thing for the Danes. It was all live music, and people who could play instruments would come play. They had a recess for food. You weren't allowed to drink in the hall.

Mother and Dad loved to dance, as did all of us kids.

Now the hall is used for receptions, birthday parties, anniversaries, etc. We even played basketball there while they were building the school. We bought Danish Brotherhood Life Insurance from a place located in Ionia. I had it all my life. Finally, there were just 27 members that still had insurance and it was decided that we would sell the DBS Hall to the Trufant Community Players, because the 27 members couldn't afford to put on a new roof, add a bathroom, and build a ramp, all necessary enhancements. We decided to sell it for a penny to the players, with the restriction that the remaining members could have lifetime use of the hall. It is still in pretty good shape. It continues to be used today and is where we have Krebs Christmas each year. This is a long-standing tradition, and we have only missed the past two years because of Covid. I chose the picture of the DBS Hall for the cover because it was woven throughout my life, and also endured many changes over the years.

The Gas Station

Gas at that time was rationed, as was sugar and rubber (tires). Gas was 19 cents a gallon, and you could only get a certain amount. People rode together and were very conscientious about saving gas.

Gas was 19 cents a gallon, and you could only get a certain amount.

The Drug Store

The Drug store was owned by Dorotha's parents, Doc and Ada Miller. Doc's father had been a pharmacist and Doc had remedies for things when people didn't need to see a doctor. Sulpha was something "prescribed" often. Ada worked at the store and liked to talk with her customers. She once asked Dad if any of his married girls were pregnant. Dad said, "I don't know, Ada, but I bet they are both exposed." She knew everything that was going on around town and was always trying to get the scoop!

You could buy a variety of things from Miller's, like food, ice cream, candy, remedies, and drinks. You could even buy dynamite! After Dad bought the lake property, they had to build a road on it and needed to get rid of the stumps. Rit was fourteen years old and Dad sent him to buy dynamite, caps, and a fuse.

The Post Office

In the early days, mail was delivered by horse and buggy or sleigh. When the weather was bad or roads were in poor shape, this was a difficult job. Dr. Bunce's daughter, Virginia (Mabel Virginia, but they called her Virginia), returned to Trufant in 1943 to become Postmaster. She served in this capacity for nearly thirty-four years, which she thoroughly enjoyed. She had me take the Civil Service exam so I could relieve her when she went on vacation. I did that several times. Virginia married (Lawrence) Hugh Rose, who worked for over twenty-five years at Federal Mogul Corp. in Greenville.

The Barber Shop

Stan Christensen was the first barber I remember. Gary Larson was the next barber but passed it on to John Quigg when he bought the Tavern. That was a great place to talk and learn what was going on around town. Ladies aren't the only ones who gossip when they got their hair done!

Cattle Barn (*now the Flea Market*)

Mom and Sarah Darling worked at the Cattle Barn. Art Petersen owned the land and had a building on it. He had the farmers bring their cattle, and then he would tag and weigh them. When he had a herd ready, he would auction them off. They used a wire rope with a cup. He put a tag in the cup and the wire took it up to the second floor. Two women looked at the tag and figured out the deal. When I came home from college, I would sometimes sub for them. Cathy has memories of watching the cup go up the wire.

When the cattle business ended, vendors started bringing things in to sell like produce, flowers, goods, etc. Eventually, Art's sons took over. It became a huge flea market that still runs today on Thursdays from April 1 to October 1. Vendors sell various items including plants, antiques, clothing, jewelry, produce, and food. It is known throughout the state. Two years ago, Paul Smith bought it and it continues to go strong today.

The School

The Blake school in Trufant was for kindergarten through 8th grade and played a large part in the Trufant community. P.T.A. (Parents Teacher Association) meetings were both a social outing and a family affair. We would discuss school business, lunch was served, and there was entertainment; I remember the parents even putting on a play! People played instruments and sang songs. We also had picnics and "box socials". You took a shoe box and decorated it and filled it with lunch items. The board members would auction the boxes and you would give clues to the one you hoped would get your box, like a friend or

Lutheran church, popular with Danes–
Dad was Lutheran but didn't practice

Logging

Downtown view

Another view of downtown with drug store on the left

someone you had a crush on. Kids and parents exchanged lunch boxes, ate, and the parents discussed issues related to school while kids played together. P.T.A. meetings were quite the event.

Kindergarten got out at noon, first grade at 1:30, and the rest at 4:00 p.m. Minnie Earl, one of the teachers, had a model A Ford and took the kindergarten kids home. She always said, "I drive safety first." After the war when times were hard, the school would provide lunch for everyone once a month. The teacher would set the soup or stew on the furnace to keep it warm, and the room would soon be filled with the fragrant, delicious smell of a hot lunch! It was hard to focus and we couldn't wait until it was time to eat.

Eighth grade graduation was a big deal because some people didn't go on to high school. Dad was on the school board and was also the Maple Valley Township Treasurer. Mom always helped him with his duties.

Believe it or not, during potato season, we actually had "potato vacation," two weeks off from school so we could help pick potatoes. We were paid two cents a bushel. In that two-week timeframe we earned enough money to buy our clothes for the winter. We loved looking at the Sears and Roebucks catalog to see what we could buy. We actually got to pick our clothes (with the help of Mom and Dad). That was a real highlight!

The Telephone

The telephone played an important role in our lives by enabling us to stay connected with our community and helping Dad in his business dealings. We had a telephone on the farm that hung on the wall. Our number was 25F-13.

The 13 signified one long ring and three short rings. We shared our phone line with neighbors, and this was a challenge. Dad used to get upset when he got long distance calls about his potato business. One lady always listened in on the phone calls, and you couldn't hear as well when someone was listening in on the line. Dad would say, "Hang up, Tillie, and I'll call you back to give you the news."

There was a telephone line man for each section of the telephone. If there was a problem, they would take care of it. There were about twenty-five families on a line.

Our Church

As kids, we went to St. Clara's Catholic Church in Maple Valley, which was later moved to Coral. The altars and pillars are still the same. There was a priest's house and a cemetery across the street. We attended catechism classes after church and during the summer. My brothers were altar boys, and they took their time finishing up at the end of mass to avoid catechism classes. We also attended St. Mary's church in Sand Lake, where LeMoyne and I would eventually be married.

Living at the convent instilled the deep Catholic faith that Mother passed on to each of us. She taught all of us our religious training, and each one of her children were baptized, confirmed, and married in the Catholic church. Dad was baptized in the Lutheran church but didn't follow his faith. He made sure mother and all of us got to St. Clara's church in Maple Valley each Sunday. On Saturday nights we all had baths in a tub with a curtain around it. Our "Sunday's best" and shoes were all laid out on Saturday night, and they were only worn to church. Mother was truly a saint on earth for getting all of us ready for church each week! The older kids got to take a sponge bath. Dad drove us in the potato truck and dropped us off until it was time to pick us back up. He often visited his friend, Glen Rowland. There was a spot in the corner of our house to kneel and pray the rosary. I have vivid memories of teaching Alger and Rit their prayers. June had a bad time when her daughter Lori was born. I remember mother asking everyone to kneel and pray for June. We often came together to pray for our friends and family.

There was another very popular church in town, the St. Thomas Lutheran Church, which is where Dad was baptized. Many of the Danish settlers attended this church. Dad did not attend church after he and mother were married.

The Doctor

Dr. Earl Bunce was married to Nettie and they had two children, Mabel Virginia Bunce (See Post Office) and Leo Bunce. They enjoyed more than fifty years together and their family was liked by everyone.

In the early years, Dr. Bunce followed his profession by horse and buggy in the summer and sleigh and snowshoe during the winter. At that time nearly all the practice was in the home, as few patients came to the office. When babies were born (mostly at home), Mother helped him deliver babies, and would stay for two days (sometimes longer) until the mother could be on her own. She was a valued resource for Dr. Bunce as he always said she was the best nurse he worked with, although she had no formal training. Dad would take care of us while Mom was gone and even cooked our meals. He would always ask, "Who is the better cook?" Ha! The answer was Mother, of course.

When Dr. Bunce retired, his son Leo took over his practice. The story goes that Leo had returned from World War II and took over his dad's practice for a week while Dr. Bunce was on vacation. He enjoyed working in his hometown and when his dad returned, they talked it over and Leo decided to stay. Earl retired in 1986. Once Frieda graduated from nursing school, she also worked for Dr. Bunce.

The Bank

Andrew Petersen, MaryAnn Petersen's dad, was the president of the bank. He seemed like a nice man, and was always well-dressed. He sometimes gave us a ride to school. We didn't know what happened, but he absconded in the night and never returned. I don't know if he took money, if there were financial problems or what really happened, but I always wondered about it. Many banks went out of business after the war. His wife brought up her four kids on her own: Eloise, MaryAnn, Nettie Jane, and Winston. Belva and Jack eventually bought Winston's house.

Trufant today, 2022

Montcalm
County Schools

This Certifies That

Margaret Mary Nielsen

is a graduate of ___Blake School___ and has complete
the studies prescribed for the first eight grades of the Public School
of Michigan and is therefore awarded this

Diploma

Given at Stanton, Michigan,   *May 29th 1936*

Dorothy Kenney
Teacher

Harold C. Reber
Commissioner

STATE OF MICHIGAN
STATE BOARD OF EDUCATION

REGISTERED KENT COUNTY
DATE *1-21-63*

ELEMENTARY PROVISIONAL CERTIFICATE

This certifies that the individual indicated below, in accordance with the provisions of Act 55 of the
Public Acts of 1935, as amended, is authorized to teach all subjects in kindergarten through grade
eight, inclusive, and to teach the following subjects in grades nine through twelve:

INST 01   KREBS, MARGARET MARY
                        NAME OF CERTIFIED

ENDORSEMENTS

All applicable codes indicated hereon are
defined on the reverse side of this certificate.

No. EPI   10350

From 07/27/62 to June 30, 1967

SECRETARY, STATE BOARD OF EDUCATION

Kent County K-12 Certificate

My Education and Career

Mother and father were always focused on furthering our education. Both parents expected us to give our best in school. We had a big blackboard on the wall in our kitchen, where we learned to write and do math. Mom said she knew I'd be a teacher because I always wanted Alger and Rit to be at the blackboard so I could teach them.

Blake School, in Trufant, was where I went from first through the eighth grade (I skipped kindergarten since I could already read.) We made our own lunches and walked to school and back every day. We often had no wax paper, so we saved bread wrappers (although we seldom bought bread) or cereal boxes to wrap our sandwiches in. We wrapped our lunches in newspapers and sacks. It was usually a sandwich and a cookie. We received milk at school.

Both parents expected us to give our best in school.

In eighth grade I was sent to Stanton to compete in a Montcalm County Spelling Bee. I competed with other girls and boys, and I won! What a happy day!! I still have the certificate!

Montcalm County Spelling Bee Champion, 1936

I started High School when I was twelve years old. Trufant's high school was just being built, so I went to Coral High School for my ninth grade year. The high school in Trufant was finished that year, so I attended Trufant high school where I finished grades 10-12. Both Belva and I played on the school softball and basketball teams. Belva was a pitcher, and I was a catcher. We both loved most sports.

We both loved most sports.

Annual Staff 1936

Earl Sorensen, Eloise Peterson, Josephine Johnson, Margaret Nielsen, Covell Olsen, Lester E. Howe, Leona Jensen, Bernice Miller, and Eula Mi...

Softball picture from yearbook

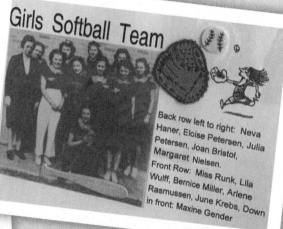

Girls Softball Team

Back row left to right: Neva Haner, Eloise Petersen, Julia Petersen, Joan Bristol, Margaret Nielsen.
Front Row: Miss Runk, Lila Wulff, Bernice Miller, Arlene Rasmussen, June Krebs, Down in front: Maxine Gender

Maple Valley School Trufant, MI

19 39

Girls Basketball Team

Left to Right: Standing: Coach Tobin, Alice Poulsen, Manager Arlene Rasmussen, Eula Miller, Madeline Clausen, Josephine Johnson, Leons Jensen, Verna Maddhes. Alice Jensen and Louise Poulsen were yell leaders.

Sitting: Pauline Kain, Wanda Lavendar, Ruth Knoft, Belva Nielsen, Eloise Petersen, Margaret Nielsen. Far right: Pauline Kain, Captain.

Basketball picture with Belva

Margaret Nielsen
Glee Club
Orchestra
Softball
Basketball
Annual Staff

High School activities

At sixteen years old, I graduated as the Valedictorian of my class and won a two-year Reader's Digest scholarship to attend Central State Teachers College (CMU). I couldn't believe it! Without the scholarship, I could have never gone to college.

Central State Teacher's College ID

Valedictorian Certificate with Reader's Digest Scholarship

May 21,   Margaret Nielsen

VALEDICTORY

There are people who always like to have the last word but to me it seems the hardest of all words to say, and I would rather someone else should be the one to say it. For the last word we must say to Classmates is "Good-Bye".

As we go forth in life after our Graduation, we feel that there are still many greater goals to reach. Each graduate will have a certain position to play in life, we feel certain he will do his part in fulfilling all responsibilities placed upon him.

We are passing out of High School into a still more active participation of life. During the school year we have learned to co-operate in work, and help each other in times of both need and pleasure. In learning these things in High School it makes us better prepared to cooperate and help others in later life.

It is not only the big things that count in life.it is the little things that make up your life. By helping everyone we can we are working the best way toward Success.

While we are studying in school sometimes we say, "What good will this do me" but in later life it will be found that it was just such a subject that helped us find our position in life. You will always need education no matter what occupation you choose.

It seems well for us who are about to step forth into the world's progress to consider what our parts in the battle of life are or ought to be, as citizens of the grandest nation in the world. We as citizens of the United States can be justly proud of our nation. Think of all the people abroad who have no land which they can call their own. They fought for their land as loyal citizens but were not successful in keeping it. So we should be happy to do everything in our power to make our nation a better one to live in. We want to make our land the ideal nation, by showing good example. Whatever elevates the lives of an individual also elevates the standards of the community in which he lives. Let us make loyalty our controlling spirit, and in being loyal to God, to ourselves, and to our school, we shall of necessity be loyal to every larger claim that the American nation can demand of us.

Teachers, you have had the training of us the past years, and have done your best to cultivate both our minds and our bodies. You have put forth every effort to make real men and women of us. How well you have succeeded only the future can determine. But we thank you for all you have done or tried to do for us.

Parents, you also deserve much credit, you have made it possible for us to go through school. You have sacrificed many of the pleasures of life to make it possible for your son or daughter to receive an education. Each one of us the graduates tonight, surely deeply appreciates what their parents have done for them. To show our appreciation to them we will to the best of our ability, try toward Success. We will climb slowly but steadily toward success enduring all heartaches and disappointments.

We have chosen the Carnation as our class flower, because it is a flower that is lasting and beautiful. In the language of flowers the Carnation typifies endurance. When it is picked and put in a vase with other flowers, it will be found fresh and beautiful long after the others have been withered and have been thrown away. Because of this we feel that it is very appropriate as a symbol of our class which has tonight finished its work in school, while others have stopped by the way and been unable or unwilling to hold on until the end of the course. So as the Carnation we will always try to brighten every corner in which we are placed.

Thus as we have learned that Success cannot be gained quickly, we must climb steadily and slowly to the top to win. It gives me great pleasure to give you our Motto "The Elevator to Success is not running Take the Stairs. I Thank You.

                                          Margaret Mary Nielsen

Valedictorian speech, 1940

Money was extremely tight since we had just lost the farm, and Mom and Dad were not going to be able to help me with school. Dad said I could pick cucumbers to earn money to start college. We took the cucumbers to Lakeview, where they were sold to the cucumber factory, and I was paid $30. I was determined that I was going to go and try to make it work. We weren't sure how I was going to get to school. Dr. Bunce offered to give me a ride, as he was going to visit his daughter, Virginia, who was already there. I could work on N.Y.A. (National Youth Asso-

Auction of family farm in newspaper

ciation), which paid $0.35 an hour. Through this program, I got a job working for a professor. I also found a bulletin board where a woman was posting rooms to rent. She asked me if I needed a place to stay and I said yes. She said I could clean ten rooms on the weekend to cover a free room that I shared with her daughter and two other students. I didn't have any money for books, so I borrowed them from people in the house, or found them at a secondhand store. These were hard times for me as my parents could not help me. Many days I did not have enough to eat. My college years were not fun, but I was very determined to get my education.

I had very few clothes. Sometimes my roommates and I exchanged clothes with each other. I walked ten blocks to buy day old bread for ten cents. I took many odd jobs. I helped a woman who was catering dinners and I helped a lady who was expecting a baby. I took every job that I could get. While we were dating, LeMoyne came to visit me when I was in college, and we went to the Sweetheart Dance together. That was a fun memory. I also worked that summer as a maid in Greenville.

I went to college for two years to get my State Limited Certificate. Then my last six weeks I had to take a bus out into the country to student teach. Although I had my driver's license, I didn't have a car to drive until I was married. My brother Rit and I had received our driver's licenses at the same time. Rit was fourteen and I was eighteen.

While I was student teaching, I couldn't work my jobs to earn any money, so I thought I was going to have to quit. I'll always be so grateful to my brother, Boots, as he was working at Waterford and said he'd loan me money to get through those six weeks. He saved my college life. What a brother!

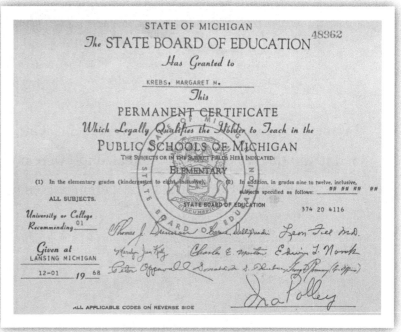

Teaching Certificate

I got my first teaching job in Pierson, where I taught 4th through 8th grades. I stayed in Pierson during the week and rode back and forth with Joe Hubbard, who was also working in Pierson. The next year, I secured a better job in Trufant School. I taught there for nine years, then moved on to Cedar Springs, where I taught for twenty-nine and a half years. For fourteen years I was a Reading Consultant in the Reading Center, teaching and running the program for remedial readers.

Teacher oath

I wanted to be a good example to my students. One of our subjects was health, and it said that tea and coffee (and alcohol) were not good for kids, so I didn't drink them either. How could I drink them but tell the kids not to? I also didn't care for the taste of alcohol.

Margaret Krebs

Teacher
of the week

Teacher of the Week at Beach Elementary School in Cedar Springs is Margaret Krebs, the reading consultant.

A graduate of Central Michigan University, she has completed graduate work at Michigan State University and studied in England one summer.

Raised in Trufant, she returned to teach there for nine years and a year in Pierson.

The past 26 years, Mrs. Krebs has taught in Cedar Springs, eight of those in remedial reading and as the reading consultant.

Mrs. Krebs' family includes five brothers, three sisters, her husband, LeMoyne, daughters, Cathy, of Greenville, Jayne, of Grand Rapids, sons Tom, of Cadillac, Dan of Houston, Texas, Alan, at home, and nine grandchildren.

Mrs. Krebs, who lives in Howard City, is on the finance committee at Christ the King Church and spends her free time playing the organ, bridge and golf, reading and traveling.

Teacher of the Week, Cedar Springs

I went on to take extensive in-person and correspondence courses to finish my Bachelor of Arts degree. It took many summers and evenings to complete my degree, which I received when I turned forty. I then began working on my Masters' degree in Reading and attended one three-week reading course in England. I stayed with Lloyd's daughter, Mary Kay. In 1986, when I was sixty-two, I retired from thirty-nine and a half years of teaching.

CMU Bachelors of Arts

College friends, including Beatrice Roller

Early pictures, tickets from first date

Keep This Coupon

35379

Good for One Chance on
Prize to be given away at
this place on the date
advertised.

Good
For

LeMoyne

It was during the tenth grade that I met the love of my life, LeMoyne Dayle Krebs, who had moved to Michigan from California. He was a freshman, one year younger, but I was sure he was the one for me. Our first date was in November. We went to the school carnival in his parent's red truck.

We dated but didn't get to see each other much since our parents were very strict. We sat together on the bus on the way to school and to basketball games. Both of us were active and good at sports. During our junior and senior years, we were able to go to Greenville to the movies, and to dances at the D.B.S. Hall.

LeMoyne and I dated on and off while I was in college. He did come take me to the Cupids Caper Ball, which was a fun memory. The summer after I graduated, we got back together. When he graduated from Trufant high school, he worked at American Seating and then at the Willow Run bomber plant, where he became a foreman at age nineteen. He always moved up quickly in his jobs.

Also at age nineteen, LeMoyne was drafted into the Navy. Before he left for boot camp, we talked about getting engaged. We drove to Greenville with our friends to shop for a wedding ring. LeMoyne purchased the ring and put it in his pocket. Arlene told LeMoyne to put the ring on my finger, but he wanted more time to prepare. Arlene persisted, and eventually LeMoyne put the ring on my finger. We were engaged. Shortly thereafter, he left for boot camp in Chicago. I had a friend whose boyfriend was at the same bootcamp, so we would travel by train to Chicago to visit them for a few hours on the weekend when they were on leave.

Margaret and LeMoyne

After my first year of teaching, Dad found a house in Trufant. He heard the lady was going to sell it and told me to go find out about it. I bought the house and two lots for $250. It needed a new roof, so Grandpa White jumped in to help. He let me pass up the shingles to him, but soon said I was moving too fast, so he had me join him on the roof. We put the roof on together. We also added cupboards, a living room, and a bathroom. Grandpa helped with everything and taught me so much. He was always there with a smile and a helping hand. That would be the first of fifteen different houses that LeMoyne and I would live in together (after we were married). He had moved often as a child, and so this didn't seem unusual for him.

During our engagement, LeMoyne was sent to Coos Bay, Oregon. We talked often by phone. One night he called at midnight (due to the time change). Dad answered because he thought something was wrong with his sons (Boots was in the Navy and Alger in the Army Airforce), but it was LeMoyne, asking if we could get married on June 6, 1944, when he'd be home on leave. Our wedding date also turned out to be a very historic date known as D Day, which marked the start of a long and costly campaign to liberate north-west Europe from Nazi occupation during World War II. As we were setting up for the wedding, Mom heard the news of the attacks at Normandy. She was worried about her boys, particularly about Boots, who was serving in

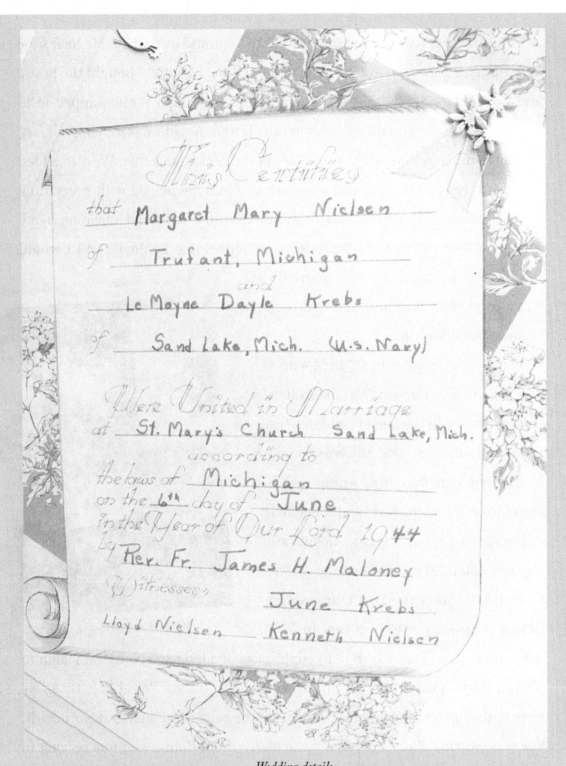

This Certifies

that **Margaret Mary Nielsen**

of **Trufant, Michigan**

and

Le Moyne Dayle Krebs

of **Sand Lake, Mich. (U.S. Navy)**

Were United in Marriage

at **St. Mary's Church Sand Lake, Mich.**

according to

the laws of **Michigan**

on the **6th** day of **June**

in the Year of Our Lord **1944**

by **Rev. Fr. James H. Maloney**

Witnesses

June Krebs

Lloyd Nielsen   Kenneth Nielsen

Wedding details

that area. We almost canceled the wedding but decided to go forward as planned. Thankfully Boots and Alger both returned home safely.

We were married at the Sand Lake Rectory since LeMoyne had not finished his instructions to become a Catholic. Since we couldn't be married in the sanctuary, we were married in the church office. LeMoyne's sister June (who ended up marrying my brother Alger) was my maid of honor and my brother Ken was the Best Man. Lloyd drove us to the ceremony and the hotel, as we had a problem getting gas rationing stamps. A big reception was held in the Trufant gym. We spent our wedding night at the Pantlind Hotel in Grand Rapids, which was considered one of the finest hotels in the country. It would receive refurbishment by the Amway Corporation and become the Amway Grand Plaza in 1981. It is still a popular hotel in downtown Grand Rapids today.

Margaret in her wedding gown

Wedding picture

After three days we left by train for Oregon with no sleeping facilities. The train was filled with sailors, wives, and friends. I'm sure you can imagine what that was like with men about to be deployed and their girlfriends and wives saying good-bye. What a revelation for a country girl like me! We had to sit up for three days. What a honeymoon!

We went to the U.S.O. in Oregon and found a couple who needed some help. I did housework and answered phones for Roy and Louise Grim. They had a mortuary and beauty shop. I stayed with LeMoyne that summer and then returned home to teach.

While LeMoyne was in the service, his mother, Hulda, passed away. Everyone was so sad as she was a wonderful woman who was loved by all who knew her.

From Oregon, LeMoyne went to Cedar Rapids, Iowa for Cadet training, where I joined him during that summer. In August, the war ended, and he was sent to California to be mustered out of the Navy. I was pregnant with Cathy, and I came home to wait for him. I taught until she was born. LeMoyne and I went on to have five children together: Cathy, Tom, Jayne, Dan, and Alan.

When LeMoyne came home, he went into business with his father at the hardware store. We got our first car, which had one seat for the driver and a crate for the passenger. He wanted a farm, so we sold our first home that Dad, Grandpa White, and I had renovated together and bought a farm on Black Road; Tom was born there. Dad and Grandpa White also helped us renovate the farmhouse. Grandpa White always loved LeMoyne, and called him, "Lee." He used to come over every Sunday to see us, and we always looked forward to that.

When Tom was very young, he was upset and said he was going to run away. We talked it over and told him that if he had to, he should do it. He packed a suitcase and started walking down the old railroad track they had taken up in later years. He was about ten years old, so we felt confident he wouldn't be gone long. Well, it was only about ten minutes before he returned. He said, "So I see you still have the same cat?" Oh, how we laughed!

Next, we bought a farm from Harry Clausen. Jayne and Dan were born there. LeMoyne milked the cows in the morning before work and I milked them after I got home from teaching. Once we had a calf coming, and LeMoyne was at work. I was trying to help the cow get comfortable and saw that the feet were coming first. I went to get Charlie Smith, our neighbor, who helped me deliver the calf. Life on the farm was always an adventure. Again, Dad helped renovate that house, but this time told LeMoyne he did not want to continue to renovate houses for him to turn around and sell.

Lemoyne Krebs awarded plaque

LeMoyne Krebs

LeMoyne D. Krebs, President of the Howard City State Bank was presented with a plaque for his services as president of the Mid-Michigan Chapter of the Banker Administration Institute for the years 1966-67.

Krebs, who has been associated with the Howard City bank for the past several years, is also a member of the Cedar Springs Rotary Club.

We moved to Howard City in 1965, when LeMoyne got a job at Western State Bank. Alan was born in Howard City that year. We built a beautiful brick house, and then LeMoyne became the President of the bank. We joined a dance club and a dinner club, and we played bridge and golf. While we were building the brick house, we lived in a cottage on Whitefish Lake. We took the children on many trips, including a big trip out west to Nebraska and South Dakota. We showed the kids where LeMoyne grew up and they met many of his relatives. Those were happy days.

Margaret, LeMoyne and Boots

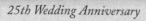
25th Wedding Anniversary

Howard City bowling league

Margaret in front of the oil well on Green Road

CHAPTER TEN

Lots of Real Estate

Over the years we had many different real estate deals, along with LeMoyne's different jobs. Some of them worked out great, while others not so much.

Little Pete's House: The first of a couple of houses that we bought and remodeled, alongside Alger and June, was Little Pete's house. Little Pete was known as the town drunk, and when he died, we bought his house. June and I remodeled it and then sold it. We had two deals with Alger and June. Around this time, LeMoyne began selling pumps.

Trufant Lake: After Little Pete's house. Alger and June, and LeMoyne and I, bought land on Trufant Lake and sold it in lots. LeMoyne was working different factory jobs during this time. We both lived there for five or six years until Alger sold his house and went to teach at Cedar Springs. We moved shortly thereafter.

Mobile Homes with Jack Edison: LeMoyne became dissatisfied with his job as bank President, and late in 1970 he left the bank and went into business with our friend, Jack Edison. He began selling mobile homes and real estate, which began a series of poor ventures.

Oil Rights: One good opportunity presented itself when Mrs. Ralph Weirkert called and asked LeMoyne if we wanted to buy twenty acres of their land. They had moved from Howard City to Florida and were not coming back. She said if we bought the land, she would also give us the oil rights. LeMoyne came and asked me because we didn't have the money at that time. He said we should borrow the money for the land because he knew he could sell it and we could keep the oil rights. I agreed, and we went to First State Bank in Greenville to get a loan to buy the land. To finalize the deal, Mrs. Weirkert also asked LeMoyne to bring his lawyer to Florida to meet with their lawyer. He agreed, and the purchase was complete. As promised, LeMoyne sold the land and kept the oil rights, which I still have today. There were several other people being paid on the same lease, but I never knew who they were. This truly was a good deal!

The well is still in use today. There are two wells on the property: a flowing well, and a capped well used for deliveries. Many years ago, I invited everyone out to see the oil well on Green Road in Reynolds Township, and we took pictures.

This truly was a good deal!

Pineview Estates: LeMoyne and Art Behrenwald bought 160 acres of land at M46 and Jones Road. Eighty acres was woods; the other land was surveyed, and roads were built to ready the plots of land, which would be called Pineview Estates. We built a house on Jones Road and 46. Our sons Dan and Alan eventually built houses on that land as well.

The Party Store: LeMoyne eventually sold the home on Jones Road and used the proceeds to build Krebs Party Store. At that time, we moved to a rental house in Howard City at 124 Lincoln Street, which we took with a mobile home deal. That is the home where I live today. The party store deal failed. At that time, LeMoyne was deeply involved with his secretary. He moved out and decided to move to Texas. He said I could not go with him.

I knew he was unfaithful, but the kids loved him, and I wanted to keep the family together. That was a very sad time not only for me, but for all my children and grandchildren. Alan was still in high school and he and I became very close. He was the most kind and helpful son I could have ever hoped for. He is still that way today. I never would have made it through without my loving family and relatives. We divorced in 1981.

Selling Pineview Estates: With LeMoyne gone, I had to handle the affairs associated with Pineview Estates. LeMoyne had sold some of the land back to Art Behrenwald and I was left to sell the remaining lots. Art's sons were now in charge and were very kind to me. I was trying to sell the lots while teaching school, and I was tired of driving out to show the lots after work and the constant inquiries about the property. Frustrated and tired, I decided to talk to a real estate agent who was interested in buying the lots. He offered me a fair price, but the Behrenwald boys didn't want me to sell to him. They offered to buy me out at the same price, so I sold the lots to the boys. I left the 80 acres of woods for Tom, Dan, and Alan, and at the same time I gave Cathy and Jayne each a lot in Florida. LeMoyne got a corner of M46 and Jones Rd. for his portion.

Christ the King & St. Francis de Sales Parish (recent picture)

Inside Christ the King & St. Francis de Sales Parish

CHAPTER ELEVEN

Founding Christ the King & St. Francis de Sales Church

In 1970, Father Bruck, a priest from the Grand Rapids Diocese, came to meet with me to discuss starting a Catholic church in Howard City. He said, "I was told I should contact you because you know all of the Catholic people!" He asked if I would help him start the church. I hosted a meeting at our home with fourteen people and Father Bruck, and he explained how we would start the new church. Everyone was excited about the prospect of the new church and agreed to help. We held masses in the Masonic Lodge and then the schoolhouse for two to three weeks until Father Bruck found a vacant Methodist church building that we could buy. It was purchased for $5,000 and later sold for $6,000. Father Bruck was a great communicator, and it didn't take long for him to fill the church with parishioners. We stayed in that church for five years, until it was bursting at the seams. In 1972, LeMoyne found seventeen acres of land that the church could buy on the corner of US 131 and

M46. St. Apollonia in Morley and St. Francis de Sales joined with us to form Christ the King and St. Francis de Sales. The church was dedicated in 1976. I am very proud to have been a part of starting this church.

> *I am very proud to have been*
> *a part of starting this church.*

There were many wonderful priests over the years. In the early years, Father Bruck, Father Witkowski, and Father Phong were strong communicators, and they were very involved in the community, which helped the church thrive.

Fr. Raymond Bruck 1970-1979, 2003-2004
Fr. Louis Anderson 1979-1982
Fr. Philip Witkowski 1982-1990
Fr. William Zink 1990-1995
Fr. Phong Pham 1995-1999
Fr. Philip Silwinski 1999-2003
Fr. Troy Nevins 2004-2007
Fr. James Wyse 2007-2016
Fr. James VanderLaan 2016-current

I met a lifelong friend through church, Noreen Gondre; we went on many fun adventures together. For several years, Noreen took me to church when I could no longer drive. When I could no longer hear what was being said, I stopped attending church and started watching mass on TV. Noreen would bring me communion at home each week but had to stop when Covid hit. Now Deacon Dubridge brings me communion, and I continue to listen to mass via TV.

Fellowship Hall recently added

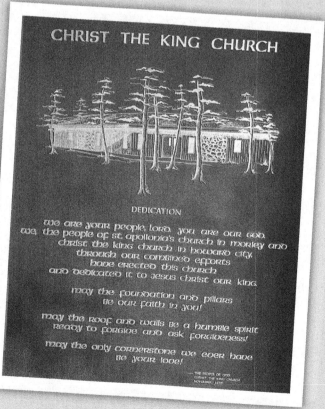

Statue of St. Mary on church grounds

Dedication plaque inside church

What happens in Vegas! Room party!

2018 Harvest Fe
Grand Marshal

Harvest Festival Grand Marshal with granddaughters, Haley and Mary

Fond Memories

I have so many fond memories to share; here are just a few.

Helping Dorotha Pike:

Dorotha Pike ran the telephone switchboard in their home for twenty-three years. She was married to Joe Pike, and Joe would step in from time to time to help Dorotha with the switchboard. They didn't have kids and wanted to adopt. One day, Dorotha got a call from Dr. Bird in Greenville that there was a baby boy available if they could come get him the next day. Dorotha called me and asked if I would come with her and hold the baby while she drove home. Just sixteen at that time, I held LaVern all the way home. Later they would also adopt a baby girl, Gracie.

Dortha on the switchboard

When Dorotha passed away, I went early to the funeral and told LaVern the story that I was the first person who got to hold him. He was so touched and asked the minister to share the story during the funeral.

Golfing on Belva's birthday

Noreen, Belva, and I went up north to Baldwin to play golf on Belva's birthday. Father Bruck had told us about a tournament in Baldwin and Belva was a great golfer, so we decided to enter the scramble for $20 apiece. We found out the rules after the scramble was over; had we known the rules, we could have used the closer tee box, and we could tee up shots other than just on the tee box. Even with those handicaps we were still able to win. We were in a hurry to get back because we had a party waiting for Belva back home, but we had to wait to collect our winnings. It was worth the wait because they had all sorts of prizes for the winners. Not only did we win $100 and a trophy, but we also received shirts, hats, a clock, and even a bag of apples. We had so much fun walking out of there with all our loot. Unfortunately, we were quite late, and people back home were a bit exasperated! There were many people there to surprise Belva, but they forgave us when we shared our story and showed everyone the success we had.

It was worth the wait because they had all sorts of prizes for the winners.

Travelling Abroad

I retired at age sixty-two in 1986 from thirty-nine and a half years of teaching. I had a group of teachers and friends who traveled together for ten years. Each year we visited a different place: London, Ireland, Italy, Greece, France, Austria, Venice (twice), and many places in the US. Alice Edison went on most all of my trips, and we also went on many adventures just the two of us. She has been a lifelong companion. Travelling with friends and family has been a highlight in my life.

Ireland: Kissing the Blarney Stone

Kilkea Castle with Sondra Nielsen, Margene Swanson, Cathy (daughter),Margaret and Ev Sorsen

Notre-Dame de Paris, Margaret and Alice

Traveling friends: Sondra, Ev, Margene, Margaret and Cathy

Traveling friends (Sondra, Ev, Margene, Margaret and Cathy) with Flat Stanley

Gondola ride in Venice

Zephyrhills, Florida

Agnes and I rented a mobile home in Zephyrhills, Florida for three months every year. Cathy (my daughter) drove with me to Florida many times to help me make the trip, but then I lost my sight and couldn't drive anymore. All our family, Rit and Jean, Jack and Belva, Frieda and Leo, Boots, Agnes, and I all stayed in Zephyrhills. We all went to church together, gambled together, socialized together, LAUGHED together and loved spending time together. Agnes and I took painting classes, played cards, danced, and traveled during our time together. When Agnes married Frank, I continued to go by myself for the next four years and stayed in the same house. I was close to 80 at that time. Rit and Jean continued wintering in Florida but everyone else stopped going. Those years were very special.

Sisters: Frieda, Margaret, Belva, Agnes in Zephyrhills, FL

Nielsen Reunions

I started the Nielsen family reunion that has been held annually for more than thirty years. Each reunion starts with a golf scramble for prizes and fun, and then all the families come together to share potluck dishes, stories, and set up fun games for the kids to play. I organized the first few reunions, then each of my siblings and their families took alternating turns organizing and hosting the reunion. We started the outings at Whitefish Lake, moved to Gowen for several years, and now join together each year at McCarthy Park, near Turk Lake. It is always so much fun to see the family expanding and enjoying each other. The recap of the golf outing is always a highlight, and there are many laughs to be shared.

Howard City's Grand Marshal

A fond memory was when I was made the Howard City Harvest Festival Grand Marshal for the 150 years celebration. We had a big party at my house that day, and I was in the parade. Many of my children and grandchildren attended, and two of my grandchildren, Mary and Haley, rode in the car with me. I received a certificate of "special tribute" from Governor Rick Snyder and his colleagues. It was such an honor. Governor Snyder wrote: "Undoubtedly, as Howard City has a rich historical past, its contemporary citizens are helping to forge its future. Margaret Nielsen Krebs, a long-time resident of Howard City, has been an active community member. As an educator, she has shaped the minds of our state's children. As a faithful disciple, she helped found the first and only Catholic parish in Howard City. Thank you for your tireless work and many contributions to Howard City and the State of Michigan."

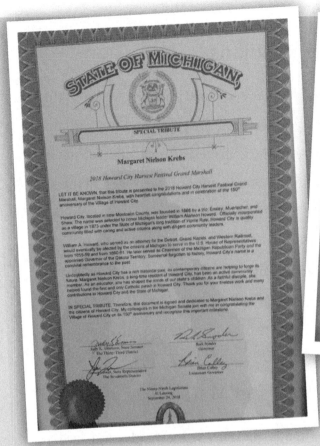

Certificate from the Governor for Grand Marshal

Daily News Article

Having a ball riding in the convertible with Alan, Haley and Mary

Picture after the parade in the backyard

Trick or Treat

I have always enjoyed passing out candy on Halloween. As I got older and was unable to see and hear people, Katie's family and Alan's family started coming over to pass out candy and spend Halloween with me (Katie Siple is my granddaughter, and Alan Krebs, my son). We have dinner together, eat a good amount of candy, and enjoy seeing the kids dressed up. Katie even brought me a costume to wear with a tiara! It has been wonderful to have Katie and Alan close by. I have had many wonderful memories with both of their families.

Josh, Addi, Mary, Margaret and Katie Siple

Margaret and Haley (Alan's daughter)

Margaret and Katie

The Mystery of Faith!

In 2021 I was visited by a mystery guest. My friend, Noreen Gondre, came by to see me. We were sitting at my table catching up on life, and I noticed someone had come into my house. I sensed it was a friendly visitor but could not tell who it was. Noreen said, "Get a little closer and see if you can tell who it is!"

I could not see him, but when he gave me a big hug, I knew exactly who it was!

Father Phong and I became good friends when he was the priest at my church, Christ the King. He was a great communicator and was very involved in the community. I was so sad when he was given a new assignment in Massachusetts. Father Phong was in Grand Rapids for a funeral. He called Doreen and told her to go to my house but to NOT tell me he was coming. What a wonderful surprise! He could only stay a short time, but we had a nice visit. I couldn't believe he drove all the way from Grand Rapids and back to surprise me. What a friend.

Heck NO! I Won't Go!

It is no secret that it has been important to me to stay in my home. I have lived in my house in Howard City for fifty-five years, and I have many fond memories here.

Current home in Howard City: 124 Lincoln St

Most of the memories are gatherings with family and friends: birthday parties, picture parties for the traveling group, the Christmas party for the reading teachers, baby showers, wedding showers, deck parties with church, family and friends, etc. My dear friend, Sharon Schwalbach, has done my hair for more than forty years. I used to go to her salon until I could no longer get out; she started coming to my house each week to do my hair. What a friend. The only way I have been able to live on my own after I became hearing and vision impaired (and could no longer drive) is because of the support from my children, family, and friends. Last year I even had a large tree fall on the front of my house and bedroom. Fortunately, I was sitting in back watching TV, so

I wasn't hurt. There was significant damage to my home, but everyone started making calls and helped get the repairs made and my yard cleaned up. There are so many people who look out for me. My children have all contributed in various ways: taking me to appointments, helping manage my finances, bringing me meals, doing projects around my house, getting my groceries, helping me plan parties, helping with yard work… these are only a few of the many things they have done. I also have numerous grandchildren, nieces, and friends who visit me, bring food, and support me in many ways. Katie has been there to find my hearing aid when I drop it, clean up spills and help do whatever I need, as well as be a constant visitor.

I must also mention Lori Cooper, who helps me each week. This is her fifth year helping me; she also helped all three of my sisters. She is willing to do anything I need and is a wonderful helper and companion. I have truly enjoyed the comfort of staying in my home.

Margaret in her praying chair

There are so many people who look out for me.

Margaret with nieces, Lori and Debby, and nephew Dirk on her deck

Margaret in her home, taking with great-grandchildren, Rachel, Kyle, Michael and Allison

One of Margaret's many beautiful Christmas cactuses

Siblings at Margaret and LeMoyne's 25th anniversary

Siblings and spouses at Tom and Cathy's 25th anniversary party

CHAPTER THIRTEEN

My Siblings

Lloyd, my oldest brother, wasn't at home when I was growing up. He seemed a little more serious and responsible as the oldest sibling but was also liked by everyone. He had a math mind. He went to Central State Teachers College for two years and taught one year at Arbogast school, north of Coral. I remember him always having patches on his pants. He was good at selling things and got recruited to work at Federal Mogul as a purchasing agent. Federal Mogel manufactured automobile parts, and he had a wonderful memory to keep track of the orders. That's where he spent the rest of his working days. Lloyd married Phylis Vanderlip and they had five children: Janet, Gerald, Mary, Karen, and Beth. They also lost one baby, Teresa.

Lloyd, high school graduation, with Frieda

Lloyd loved to tell the story that he fondly remembers Dad telling him he didn't have to do chores on his birthday, and instead he could go fishing. Lloyd loved to play bridge, and amazingly, he got a masters in bridge, which was almost unheard of in those days. He had to travel all over (even Hawaii) to get the points to get this degree. He was also an avid golfer. When his kids were quarreling, he would tell them, "I'm going to order a pizza and put you all in it!" He enjoyed taking his bag of nickels to the casino. He called me to drive him to Mt. Pleasant to gamble several times when he could no longer drive. Lloyd was a wonderful brother.

Ken was very cheerful, and well-liked by everyone. He left home to live with a family friend, Gertrude Morris, and worked at their creamery while he went to school. He picked up milk from the farmers and took it to the creamery. He did a great deal of work farming in his younger years, and eventually moved into selling cars. He was very generous even when money was scarce. He would always give us a nickel when we saw him. He was very outgoing and always popular with the girls!

Ken married Neva Kanuph and they had three daughters: Patricia, Nancy, and Mary. They lived in Trufant in a house where I previously lived. When

Nancy was born, it had been a muddy March. Ken had driven a milk truck and it was his misfortune to tip the truck over, so he was banged up and resting in bed. There was a blizzard and it was hard to keep the house warm. Dr. Haze from Howard City came to deliver the baby, and as soon as he walked in the door he said, "Get some heat in this house!" Ken got out of bed so Neva could deliver the baby. Ken said the stove was red hot but the doctor complained about the cold bedroom. Both grandmas (Belva and Daisy) held oil lamps for the doctor. They were shaking from the cold and nervous about the delivery, and at 5:05 a.m. Nancy was born. She was rushed to the living room to the stove to get warm. The doctor exclaimed that she "came in on the 505!" That was the time the train came through Howard City! They all had a good laugh.

Their youngest daughter, Mary, was hit by a car when she was about three years old. Grandma Nielsen had done the laundry, and Mary and Pat were walking a few blocks bringing the laundry home. Mary saw Dad and ran toward him, right in front of a car. She had a big gash on her head and a spiral fracture in her leg. Pat slept in bed with her; it was very scary to see her with a big bandage on her head and a huge cast on her leg. Later in life, Mary would have back surgery. When she came out of the anesthetic her heart stopped and she went blind. She had to have a lot of therapy and never could see that well again. She recognized people by their voices. She played bingo on large cards. When they were driving places, Nancy would say, "Mary, you watch for the deer!" Mary would reply, "I will!"

Ken and Neva worked at Federal Mogul where they both retired. Ken loved watching the news and always knew what was going on in the world. He had diabetes and lost his leg in 1977. I loved to visit him because he was always cheerful and had lots of company. He died in 1978. He was a wonderful brother.

Autograph books: 1931

Frieda

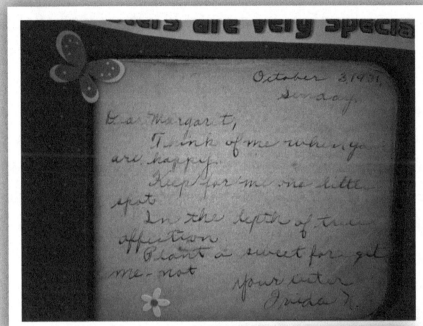

Ken

October 3, 1931,
Sunday

Dear Margaret,
Think of me when you
are happy.
Keep for me one little
spot
In the depth of true
affection
Plant a sweet for get
me - not
your sister
Frieda K.

Pierson Mich.
October 4, 1931

Dear sister Gret
When upon this page
you look,
Remember it was your
brother who wrote this in
your book.

Kenneth Nielsen

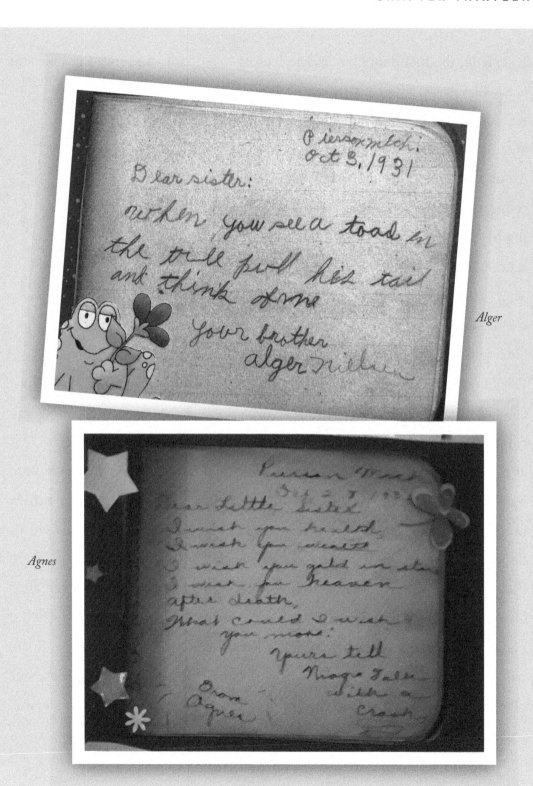

Alger

Agnes

Frieda, the first daughter, had a pleasing personality and loved to joke and tease. She was a gifted pianist and was able to take lessons at a young age. She had an excellent ear for music and could play any song we requested, reading music or playing by ear. She went to Coral high school where she met Clair Feutz. They were married and had five children together: Gerald "Lum", Norman, Alice, Jim, and Judy. Frieda graduated with the first class of nursing students at Mont-

calm Community College and worked for Greenville Memorial Hospital as well as for Dr. Bunce in Trufant. She also took care of my children when they were babies while I was teaching school. Clair died quite young, and later Frieda married Leo Kaiser, a farmer whom she met at the DBS Hall. They went to dance each week, played cards, and had a home in Zephyrhills, Florida where they spent the winter months. They also took many trips together. Even after losing her sight in her later years, Frieda lived alone and continued to play the piano, right up until she died. She also played cards with her family, and she would win! She was an avid Detroit Tigers fan and loved to talk with me about players and strategy. She died of a heart attack at the age of ninety-six. She was a wonderful sister.

Agnes was such a hard worker. As a child, I remember Agnes and Frieda were very close. I remember how much I wanted to listen to them tell secrets! Agnes had incredible vision and could easily find four-leafed clovers. One time Dad lost a key in the barn, and he woke Agnes up in the night to help him look for it. Wouldn't you know, she found it laying in the hay! Agnes graduated from Trufant high school and worked for the Cartier and Bissell families, cleaning and helping with their children. Agnes married Harold Ludke and they had eleven children. Harold's

parents gave them land and a house when they got married, and Harold and Agnes inherited the family farm when his parents passed away. They enjoyed

fishing and deer hunting together. Agnes was a very talented artist, painting beautiful pictures. She also made fresh bread each day (just like Mom) and raised eleven kids who have all done well. Her children were: Barb, Carol, Louise, Ted, Bill, JoAnne, Ed, Mark, Chris, Patricia, and Brian. Harold died of a heart attack when he was in his fifties.

Agnes and I traveled to Zephyrhills and rented a mobile home together for twenty years. We took painting classes, went dancing, and played cards. Our whole family went to Florida during those years. We also enjoyed gambling together. Later in life she married her childhood friend, Frank Skorka, and they had a great marriage. He was Catholic and went to church every day. Agnes spent five years in Lakeview Terrace nursing home, where Belva joined her and helped care for her in her final years. She was 101 when she died. She was a wonderful sister.

Carl wanted to be like his brothers when he was very young. He wanted to work in the barnyard, but in order to do that he needed boots. He was so happy when he got his own pair that the nickname stuck. He was always a playful child and loved playing tricks on people. He loved stealing our food while we were eating meals. One time he took a banana from Alger at the dinner table and Dad threw a glass of water on him. All he said was, "That felt good!"

Boots had colds and coughs and they held him back because he got sick quite often. Belva and Boots were in school together because of that. I remember one time when Mom and Dad had gone away. Boots decided he would make us some candy. It turned out green.

He said, "Well, I thought I had to put bacon powder to make it thick." We threw it out! That was Boots. He would try anything.

That was Boots. He would try anything.

Upon graduation, Boots went into the Navy and became a medic. He was in the sea of Normandy, and we all worried about him until he returned home safely after the war. He married Jeanette Corey and had three children: Ron, Steve, and Julie. He attended Central State Teacher's College on the GI bill, and upon graduation became the principal of Trufant High School. He moved to Cedar Springs High School to become the principal and worked there until he retired. He was loved by students, teachers, and parents alike, and upon retirement the school had a big celebration for him. At that time Alger was also a shop teacher and coach, and I was the reading consultant, so the three of us were all working at Cedar Springs and drove to school together. Sadly, Jeanette was young when she died of cancer. Boots had a home in Zephyrhills when he retired and married Dee Apsey. They had a home on Trufant Lake. Boots eventually went blind and was also diagnosed with cancer; he died at age eighty-four. He was a wonderful brother.

Belva and I were close growing up. She was a great student and athlete, and liked music. She played the violin in high school. She won the Maple Valley Spelling Bee in middle school. Upon graduation from high school, Belva married Jack Stout. He worked for a farmer when they first got married. They bought a nice house in Detroit, and Jack worked on airplanes for a year but eventually moved back to be closer to family during the war. They went back to farming (for fifty years) and had eight children: John, Joyce, Ruth, Mike, George, Cindy, Jean, and Joe. Jean and Joe were twins, and Jack teased me about whether or not I hoped she would have a boy or girl. Of course I said I didn't mind either way. He said, "Well, we got BOTH!" Cindy was just 18 months older than they were, and Joyce was like a mother to them.

When the war ended, Boots and Alger talked about how Jack was working out in the field, and they went to find him to tell him the war had ended. He was so relieved. Belva and Jack built a beautiful home in Trufant where they lived their entire life. They were honored as the master and mistress of ceremonies of the Trufant Jubilee. Jubilee tradition is to enter your house/yard in the "most beautiful" contest. You had to have a stump fence and a marigold in your yard to be considered for this award. Belva and Jack won several times and always had a beautiful yard and home. They were also known for their delicious Maple Syrup, which everyone loved. Belva also enjoyed deer hunting with Jack and was an excellent golfer.

Belva and Jack traveled to Alaska and many other places, and they bought a mobile home in Zyphryhills where the other Nielsens were living at that time. They lived there in the winter, and that was where Jack passed away. Belva came back and now she is 99 and lives in Lakeview Terrace Assisted Living, where Agnes had also lived (until she was 101). I am so happy to still have my sister to talk with most every day.

I am so happy to still have my sister to talk with most every day.

Sharing stories for the book

Margaret and her sister, Belva

Karen, Margaret, Belva and Cindy Venus

Alger was a hard-working, fun-loving brother. He was a talented athlete and loved to play baseball and basketball. He was small but fast, and Dad would tell us he could dribble through his opponent's legs. I remember when we walked to school, Alger would throw stones at the receptors on the phone lines. Unfor-

tunately, he got into trouble for being too accurate! When he finished high school, Alger went into the Army Air Corp. When he returned, he married June Krebs (LeMoyne's sister) and they moved to Mt. Pleasant where he went to Central State Teacher's College on the GI bill. Alger and June had nine children: Marilyn, James, Peggy, Suzy, Debby, Ellie, Richard, Lori, and Pat. He taught in Ashley for seven years, which is when we all bought the land at Trufant Lake and developed and sold ten lots. Alger and June, and LeMoyne and I lived there, a house apart, for about ten years. Then Alger and June moved to Cedar and LeMoyne and I moved to Howard City, selling our houses. Alger's oldest daughter, Marilyn, died of Lupus when she was just twenty years old. That was a sad time for everyone, particularly Cathy. Marilyn was her best friend. Alger was a respected teacher and coach until retirement. He had many winning teams and was well-loved by the Cedar community (his daughter, Peggy and granddaughter, Lynnette would also teach there). Sadly, June passed away from Parkinson's. Later Alger married Nancy Kehoe and they did a great deal of traveling; they loved going to Texas for the winter. Alger loved working in his garden, and even planted potatoes using his "antique" potato planter. He had a heart attack in his garden, which seemed fitting that he was doing what he loved. We all miss him.

Margaret and June Krebs, LeMoyne's sister who would later marry Margaret's brother, Alger

My Dear Baby Sister:

Congratulations on your reaching another milestone in your journey thru life.

I remember you as a cute three year old slightly spoiled by all of us.

Then grade school where you were very precocious.

After High School where in addition to academic ability you also excelled in music + softball. You also did a lot of Baby sitting for Ossie + Irene.

By that time I was teaching and didn't see much of you.

Your teaching career was a great success and your ready smile, (and laugh) and friendship to all, added to your popularity.

May your future be blessed with good health, happiness and luck with the One Armed Bandits.

Lloyd.

P.S. See Envelope

Precious letter from my brother, Lloyd.

Letter from Lloyd on Margaret's 70th birthday

*Margaret with dear friends
Jack and Winnie Edison*

*Margaret and Leo Kaiser
(Frieda's second husband)*

Rit was the baby of the family but was determined to keep up with his siblings. He was a sweet boy and was given a great deal of attention from his sisters. He was a talented athlete and good at any sport. Besides his love of baseball, he raced stock cars, and beat many talented drivers from neighboring cities. Rit was also always working. He helped Alger run the farm at just thirteen years old, and he continued to work on neighboring farms while so many were away in the service. Rit also worked at the cement block plant for Ed Williams, which was hard work, but he made great money. He played baseball after high school and was a talented pitcher. Many teams wanted him on their roster. In 1950, at age 22, Rit joined the Army and was sent to Fort Benning, Georgia, for training. He was deployed to Germany for a year and a half before being discharged. When he came home, he went to work at Federal Mogul, where he met Jean Olmstead who also worked there. They were married on November 14, 1953, and they will celebrate their 69th anniversary later this year. They had six children: Dirk, Sandy, David, Larry, Bill, and Marsha. They still live in Trufant today. I am grateful for the many years I have had with Rit and Jean.

Margaret and Rit, winning big!

Rit, Jean, Alice Edison, Dirk, and Margaret working on the book

Margaret and Jean (Rit's wife)

Margaret and Rit

Cathy, Tom, Jayne, Alan, Margaret and Dan at Melissa's wedding

Margaret with her children: Jayne, Dan, Margaret, Tom, Cathy, Alan

CHAPTER FOURTEEN

MY CHILDREN:
Cathy, Tom, Jayne, Dan and Alan

Of all the adventures I have had in my life, I am most proud of my children. They have gone on to have beautiful families of their own and have been very good to me throughout my life. We currently have 69 members in our family with three more on the way. My children, grandchildren, and great grandchildren have been my greatest blessing.

Cathy worked at Old Kent Bank in Greenville for nineteen years, the last eight as branch manager. Her husband, Tom, worked at Greenville Tool and Die, and was part owner with his brother, John, at Edmore Tool and Grinding. They are proud parents of Rob (Karen) and Kelly (Brandon) and have thoroughly enjoyed retirement. Their grandchildren are Amanda, Evan, Rachel, Allison, Kyle, and Michael.

Tom married Dianna Brecker. They were proud parents to two daughters, Kristi (Frank) and Melanie (Rex). Tom was in the Navy and went to Ferris State College (now University) on the GI Bill. He graduated with a degree in business, and became a manager for Michigan Airgas, where he worked until retirement. His grandchildren are Shane, Courtney (Zach), and Olivia (Jeremy). Now there are three great-grandchildren: Remington, Oaklynn, and Benjamin. In 2016, Tom had a massive heart attack and died when he was sixty-five years old. He is dearly missed.

Jayne has been a daycare provider working from her home for forty-six years and counting. Her husband Dennis worked and was an owner with Carbide Specialties and has worked at various dealerships over the years. They are proud parents of four children: Kara (Tim), Sheryl, Melissa (Joe), and Denny, as well as seven grandchildren: Devin, Chase, Joshua, Noah, Lauren, Brenna, and Madison.

Dan was the manager of several Ford dealerships. He married Jeanine Sagorski, a wonderful cook and homemaker, who also worked in daycare. They raised four kids: Katie (Josh), Tony (Heather), James (Melanie), and Danielle (Taylor) and are now thoroughly enjoying retirement. They are also very proud grandparents to Mary Elizabeth, Braylan, Addisyn, Gabriella, Kylah, Anthony Ford, Layla, and Broox.

Alan attended Aquinas College and graduated from Ferris State University. He has worked for Bissell Homecare for twenty-three years and is currently a Principal Engineer. His wife, Heather, also graduated from Ferris State University. She is currently a fraud investigator and has worked for the State of Michigan for more than twenty-nine years. They are counting down the days until retirement! They have three children: Ryan (Brenda), Jeff (Brittny) and Haley. They are also proud grandparents to Jayden, Isabella, and Eden; baby Emma is forever in our hearts.

Margaret, Jayne, and Dan on Easter

Margaret and LeMoyne, Tom, Dan, Jayne and Cathy

Margaret and Tom, graduation

Margaret and LeMoyne, Tom, Cathy, Dan and Jayne

Margaret, LeMoyne at their 25th anniversary party with Cathy and Tom Cornell, their kids Rob and Kelly, Tom, Jayne, Dan and Alan

Margaret, LeMoyne, Tom, Dianna (Tom's wife), Cathy, Dan, Jayne and Alan (Tom's graduation)

Tom and Cathy's 25th wedding anniversary party with Margaret, LeMoyne and their children

Margaret, LeMoyne and their five children

Margaret and Dan

Tom, Alan, Dan, Jayne, Margaret, Cathy on
Easter at Tom and Cathy's

Alan and Margaret

Margaret with children, grandchildren and great grandchildren before her surgery, at her house

Margaret (age 86) with her grandchildren Margaret (age 86) with her children

Cathy, Jayne, Alan, Dan and Tom with Margaret

Margaret reviewing the book (using her magnifying glass)

Acknowledgments

Thank you to everyone who contributed to this book.

Nancy Nielsen, Debby Gingrich, Jayne Cotten, and Alice Edison for sharing pictures, newspaper clippings, stories and various documents.

Belva Stout, Cindy Venus, Rit and Jean Nielsen, and Pat Bucholtz for sharing stories.

Rob Cornell, Cathy Cornell and Jayne Cotten for helping with editing.

We also contacted the Montcalm County Michigan Geneology on the Web, for permission to use pictures prior to 1930.

Margaret saying a prayer before dinner at Rob and Karen's wedding

About the Author

Margaret Krebs resides in Howard City, Michigan, where she has lived for fifty-five years. She enjoys listening to audio books, cheering on the Detroit Tigers, and visiting with family and friends. She is now legally blind and hearing impaired, which led to her having Karen help write this book.

Karen Cornell lives in Grand Rapids, MI with her husband of twenty-six years, Rob (they were married on Margaret's 72nd birthday). She grew up in Battle Creek, graduated from Kellogg Community College (Associates of Arts degree) and Central Michigan University with a Bachelor of Science in Accounting. She worked at First of America Bank and then as a business consultant for Arthur Andersen in Houston, Texas, before staying home with her four children: Rachel (22), and triplets Allison, Kyle, and Michael (17). She loves spending time with family and friends, walking her dog, Sami, exercising, cooking, and enjoying the outdoors. Writing this book with grandma was truly a highlight of her life.

Made in the USA
Coppell, TX
28 July 2023

19679366R00083